CW01150100

YUANMINGYUAN GARDEN

圆明园

FOREIGN LANGUAGES PRESS BEIJING

外文出版社　北京

YUANMINGYUAN GARDEN

Yuanmingyuan in the western suburb of Beijing is the collective name for the Garden of Perfection and Enlightenment (Yuanmmingyuan), Garden of Eternal Spring (Changchunyuan) and Garden of Beautiful Spring (Qichunyuan). Covering 350 hectares of land and unrivalled in landscape architecture, Yuanmingyuan was the secondary palace of the Qing rulers. Its construction was undertaken by pooling manpower and materials of the whole country and continued for more than 100 years. The garden had followed and carried forward the fine Chinese traditions in landscape gardening of the previous 2,000 years and incorporated the best of the northern and southern styles of gardens. The sky and earth were represented in miniature, and palace halls, terraces and waterside pavilions stood in picturesque surroundings. The elegant scenery of the regions of rivers and lakes in the south existed side by side with the majestic mountains and rivers of the north. The garden which represented and embodied the highest aesthetic realm of Chinese culture and landscapes was a great masterpiece of landscape architecture in imperial gardens at the end of the feudal society and occupied an important place in the history of landscape architecture of the world.

First built at the beginning of the 18th century, Yuanmingyuan was originally a garden given by Emperor Kangxi (reigning 1662-1722) to his fourth son, Yinzhen. After ascending the throne, Yinzhen started in 1725 a large-scale expansion of the garden and added on the southern side the areas known as "Justness and Honesty" and "Diligent in Government and Friendly to the Virtuous," so that he could live and hold court in the garden. As a result, Yuanmingyuan became a political centre outside the Forbidden City, where many historic decisions were made and historical events took place. It was also a place where many seasonal festivities and celebrations were held. During the reigns of Emperors Yongzheng, Qianlong, Jiaqing, Daoguang and Xianfeng, over a period of 150 and more years, it had become a custom for the emperor to live, handle state affairs and give audience to ministers in the garden. On several occasions, Emperor Qianlong and Jiaqing received envoys from Portugal, the Netherlands, Britain and other European countries in the garden. Yuanmingyuan was, therefore, a garden of special significance in China's modern history.

The reign of Emperor Qianlong (1736-1795) saw the last prosperous period of the feudal society in China when Yuanmingyuan was at the zenith of its glory. As the ruler of a flourishing age, Emperor Qianlong said complacently, "I cannot forget the joy I find in natural scenery," and extensively embellished the garden. In addition to completing the 40 sights in the garden which had already taken shape at Emperor Yongzheng's time, he annexed the Garden of Eternal Spring in the east and the Garden of Beautiful Spring in the southeast. He also enlarged one after another the Serene and Clear Garden (Jingmingyuan) at the Hill of Jade Spring (Yuquanshan), the Serene and Comfortable Garden (Jingyiyuan) at the Fragrant Hill (Xiangshan) and the Garden of Clear Ripples (Qingyiyuan) by the Longevity Hill (Wanshoushan) (today's Yiheyuan, or Summe Palace), which, together with the Garden of Cheerful Spring (Changchunyuan) built at Emperor Kangxi's time, were known as the Three Hills and Fiver Gardens. By the mid-18th century, there had come into existence in the northwestern suburb of Beijing a magnificent scenic area centred around the three gardens of Yuanmingyuan. As a whole, Yuanmingyuan reflected the culture, art and productive forces of China's feudal society at the highest level and represented the highest standard of scenic construction in the cities and the art of China's landscape architecture in imperial gardens in the 18th century. Yuanmingyuan soon became famous also to the West and was praised as "the garden of gardens" and "a model the art of landscape architecture as a whole in China."

Yuanmingyuan was a large man-made garden with water in it built on level ground. In overall arrangement, it adopted the artist method of "representing the large with the small" in the traditional scholar's gardens. While creating scenic views by rearranging water and hills, it had recreated a epitomized view of the world as imagined by the ancients in China.

"Clear Sky over Nine Prefectures" (Jiuzhouqingyan) in the palace area was a scenic area with the Rear Lake at the centre. The nine islets near the edge of the lake represented "the nine prefectures demarcated by Yu, the reputed founder of the Xia dynasty" and symbolized the unification of the country.

The Lake of Blessing (Fuhai), dug in the first year of Emperor Yongzheng's reign (1723-1735), was the largest body of water in the garden. The "Jasper Terrace on Penglai Island," built at the centre of the lake, stood for the three fairy mountains of Penglai, Fangzhang and Yingzhou in the sea in fairy tales. The Lake of Blessing represented the East Sea.

"Purple and Green Mountain Lodge" (Zibishanfang) built on a hill of rocks in the northwestern corner of the garden was the commanding height in the garden and represented the Kunlun Mountains in the western part of the world in fairy tales. The man-made elevations with trees on them undulated like wooded hills in nature against a background of mountain peaks in the west. Water in clear, winding streams meandered through valleys and plains from west to east and connected the lakes and ponds into a variegated and complete water system. As the water flew around the hills and through open ground, the surface of the water narrowed and broadened and became now secluded and now exposed, creating infinite changes in atmosphere with mountains beyond mountains and placid streams. The scenery was not natural but better than that found in nature.

During the most flourishing period, there were more than 100 scenic sights, gardens within the garden, palace halls and temples in Yuanmingyuan. They represented all the basic structures in ancient Chinese architecture, such as halls, gardens, temples, village houses and market places. In architectural forms, they embraced almost all the possible plane layouts and structural shapes in ancient Chinese architecture. There were not only buildings with a single-eaved flat roof, but also palace-style buildings with multi-eaved roofs of glazed tiles. There were not only regular courtyards with one main building and two side buildings or two main buildings and four side buildings, but also complexes of garden buildings which were varied and unconfined in architectural composition. In addition to the usual rectangular, square, round, I-shaped, A-shaped, hexagonal and octagonal buildings, there were also the rare cross-shaped, enclosed-square, four-square, Buddhist-swastika-shaped, T-shaped, triangular, double-lozenge, crescent and fan-shaped buildings. The Palace of Peace and Blessing (Anyougong) built for holding memorial ceremonies for Emperor Kangxi and Yongzheng was a neatly arranged and magnificent structure. The Garden of Luxuriance (Qianyuan) was a copy of the gardens in Yangzhou. The pavilions and terraces of uneven height and different styles and shapes with trees, rocks, bird houses and flowering plants between them formed distinctive scenic zones and a colourful landscape architectural complex. Gardens and structures like these, either hidden behind hillocks, standing on hill tops or by the waterside, were gardens within the garden and turned Yuanmingyuan into a garden of infinite interest.

The scenic sights created in Yuanmingyuan embodied a diversity of themes, ranging from political and Confucianist teachings and religious supplications to aspects of life of the ordinary folk, covering everything in heaven and the human world. The largest number of them were imaginative towers and pavilions on fairy mountains, recreations of the scenery depicted in ancient poems and paintings and abstractions of natural scenery and famous and historical sites. Among the 40 scenic sights were the "Sound of Lute on Stream-Flanked Lake," which was based on the two lines of a poem by the great poet Li Bai of the Tang dynasty: "The mirror-like pond is flanked by two streams, where the twin bridges arch like rainbows"; "Spring at Wuling" reproduced the haven of peace described in the "Notes on the Land of Peach Blossoms" written by Tao Yuanming of the Jin dynasty; the "House of Apricot Blossoms in Spring" recreated the mood of the poem "Clear and Bright" by Du Mu of the late Tang dynasty; the "Light of the Sky High and Low" represented the majesty of the Yueyang Tower at Lake Dongting described in the "Notes on the Yueyang Tower" by Fan Zhongyan of the Song dynasty; the "Jasper Terrace on Penglai Island" with the imaginative "five gilded courtyards and 12 jade towers," imitated the gold-and-green style of landscape painting created by Li Sixun, a painter of the Tang dynasty; the "Vistas of Sea and Mountains" was a round marble terrace in a pond of water with a triple-eaved tower on it, which looked like a distant mirage on the sea and the land of the immortals. There were others, such as the "Distant Northern Mountain Village," which was based on Wang Wei's pastoral poems which emphasized the importance of farming; "Sitting on a Stone by a Stream," which imitated the elegant Lanting Pavilion in Shaoxing; the "Market Street," which was really like a bustling market. The "Moonlit Dwelling in Cloud" was the pure land of the Buddha echoing with the sound of chanting of Buddhist scriptures. There were a great many more of scenic sights like these in the garden, which made Yuanmingyuan indeed a garden of gardens.

Emperor Qianlong made six trips to the Yangtze Delta and bid the painters who travelled with him to draw pictures of all the scenic sights he favoured during the journey and had them reproduced in the imperial garden. The most famous ones were the 10 scenic sights of the West Lake in Hangzhou, which retained their original names when they were recreated in Yuanmingyuan. The "Likeness Garden," "Garden of Reflections," "Lion Wood" and "Little Sky Garden" in the Garden of Eternal Spring were copies respectively of the Zhan Garden in Nanking, Qu Garden in Yangzhou, Lion Wood in Suzhou and Heyan in Hangzhou. The "Study of Four Accords" in Yuanmingyuan was later renamed "Garden of Gentle Ripples" because it was a copy of the Garden of Gentle Ripples in Ninghai. These gardens in the garden were copies in essence of the originals and recreations with careful considerations of what to take and what to reject according to specific conditions. They had raised the art of landscape architecture in imperial gardens in the north to a new level. Between 1747 and 1783, a group of European-style palace buildings with fountains, popularly known as Western Buildings, were built in the northern part of the Garden of Eternal Spring. These buildings, designed by Guiseppe Castiglione (1688-1766, an Italian), Michel Benoit (1743-1774, a French), Jean-Denis Attiret (1702-1768, a French) and other European missionaries, furnished the first instance of large-scale introduction of Western garden buildings in the history of Chinese landscape architecture and a noteworthy page in the history of cultural and architectural exchange between East and West.

Flowers and trees grew luxuriantly in Yuanmingyuan and created different atmospheres as the seasons alternated at the scenic spots. Many of the scenic spots were named after plants, such as the "Peony Terrace," "Peach Blossom Yard," "Water Chestnut and Lotus Fragrance," "Kafirlily Study" and "Willow-Shaded Reading Room." Plums from the south and mimosa from the West were cultivated in the garden. Wandering among the luxuriant trees and flowers were a countless number of rare creatures like white monkeys, David's deer, cranes. peacocks and swans as well as gold fish of all colours in the lakes and ponds, which formed an organic part of the scenic sights. Yuanmingyuan during the most flourishing period was like an imperial zoo and botanical garden in the 18th and 19th centuries.

Yuanmingyuan was also the most important imperial museum and library in the whole country. Displayed and stored in the beautifully decorated and elegantly furnished halls and rooms were the most valuable books, paintings and calligraphic works of various dynastic periods together with jade articles, porcelain ware, bronzes, cloisonne, clocks and other rare treasures from all parts of the country and the world. There were also a countless number of gold and silver articles, pearls, precious stones, silks and satins, embroidered brocades, clothes, hats, personal ornaments,furniture, toys and curios.

A copy each of the *Complete Library of the Four Divisions of Books and Digest of the Complete Library of the Four Divisions of Books,* the largest collections of books in the world at the time compiled during the Qianlong reign, were stored respectively in the Pavilion of Literary Source in the Garden of Perfection and Enlightenment and the Weiyu Study in the Garden of Eternal Spring. *The Calligraphic Copybook of Chunhua Study Recarved with Imperial Approval* was carved on stone and inlaid on the corridor walls of Chunhua Pavilion in the Garden of Eternal Spring. The carving was so perfect that it was unexcelled by that of the famous *Calligraphic Copybook of Sanxitang* in Beihai's Yuegu Pavilion. The Buddha's City in Yuanmingyuan was a treasure house of Buddhist art, where thousands of gold, silver and bronze statues, gold pagodas and images as well as Buddhist scriptures were stored.

Yuanmingyuan, where the wisdom of innumerable engineers and artisans was embodied, was a symbol and epitome of the ancient civilization of the Chinese nation.

Starting from the reign of Emperor Daoguang (1821-1850), the country was increasingly crippled by social crisis, and the Qing government was increasingly straitened in finance. But Emperor Daoguang still exerted every effort to keep Yuanmingyuan in shape by dispensing with the furnishing of the Three Hills and stopping the annual autumn hunting. Although the expense involved could not be compared with that of the time of Emperors Qianlong and Jiaqing, it still exceeded 100,000 ounces of silver a year. Even on the eve of the destruction of the garden, Emperor Xianfeng still ordered the construction of the Hall of Clear Light. This showed how important Yuanmingyuan was as the political centre of the time and how valuable Yuanmingyuan was to the Qing emperors.

When the Second Opium War broke out in 1856, the Qing government dilly-dallyed between war and peace and lost several favourable opportunities. Eventually, as the British and French Allied Army advanced, the Qing army retreated again and again in defeat. Emperor Xianfeng fled to Rehe in September 1860. In October, Yuanmingyuan was plundered and set to fire by the British and French troops. Within a few days, the cultural artifacts and treasures in the garden which had been accumulated in the course of several generations were almost totally robbed or destroyed. The tragic destruction of the famous garden was a catastrophe in the modern history of civilization of China and the world.

During the reign of Emperor Tongzhi (1862-1874), Empress Dowager Cixi planned a partial restoration of Yuanmingyuan, but had to give up halfway because of exhausted financial resources.

In 1900, when China was invaded by the allied army of Eight Powers, the capital was thrown into chaotic confusion. The few structures and ancient and famous trees in Yuanmingyuan that had survived destruction were thoroughly destroyed. With the downfall of the Qing regime, the carved stones, exotic rocks, bricks and tiles at the ruins were stolen, sold or put to other use in large quantities. Millet and wheat began to grow on the site and gradually turned the garden of gardens into wilderness. The prosperity and decline of the famous garden indirectly reflected the history of rise and fall of the Qing dynasty.

Today, the ruins of Yuanmingyuan have become a symbol of China's modern history. The glory and splendour of yesterday can no longer be found on the lakes and among the trees. There are only the broken walls and columns of the Western Buildings and other ruins for people to ponder on the past. In the misty dusk, autumn breeze and spring rain, they provide much space for people's imagination. "Close to a sunken ship, a thousand sails scud by." Today's Yuanmingyuan, with its unique tragic beauty and sense of history, reminds people of the past and urges them to study the rise and fall, order and disorder of a nation. The soul-stirring power embodied in Yuanmingyuan and its special historic place are far more than what are to be found in the ruins of an imperial scenic garden.

圆 明 园

　　圆明园位于北京西郊，是圆明、长春、绮春三园的统称。它总面积350公顷，是清朝统治者集中全国人力物力，历时百余年兴建的一座规模空前的山水离宫。圆明园继承和发展了中国两千年的优秀造园传统，融汇南北园林艺术精华，移天缩地，在如画的山水环境中缔构宫室台榭，寓江南水乡之明秀于北国山川之雄奇，代表性地体现了中国人文山水的崇高美学境界，是封建社会末期皇家宫苑的集大成之作，在世界造园史上也占有重要地位。

　　圆明园始建于18世纪初，原是康熙皇帝（1662－1722年在位）第四子胤禛的赐园。胤禛即位后，自1725年起大规模增修扩建，并在园南添置朝署"正大光明""勤政亲贤"一区，园居听政。使圆明园成为紫禁城外的政治中心，许多历史决策及事件均发生在这里，岁时庆典亦多于此举行。雍正、乾隆、嘉庆、道光、咸丰五朝皇帝，前后150余年，园居成为宫廷风尚。清帝长年在园中处理政务、接引群臣，乾隆、嘉庆还数次在园内会见葡萄牙、荷兰、英国等欧洲使节，使圆明园在中国近代史上独具特殊意义。

　　乾隆朝（1736—1795年）是中国封建社会最后一个繁荣时期，也是圆明园的鼎盛时期。作为盛世君主，乾隆自诩："山水之乐不能忘于怀。"在大肆钟事增华圆明园，完成了雍正时即已初具规模的"四十景"同时，更于东邻别创长春园，于东南并入绮春园。又先后扩建玉泉山静明园、香山静宜园、创建万寿山清漪园（今颐和园），连同康熙时经营的畅春园，合称为"三山五园"。至18世纪中叶，京城西北郊形成了以圆明三园为核心的蔚为大观的风景园林之海，它们作为一个整体，反映了中国封建社会末期社会文化、艺术和生产力的最高水平，代表着中国18世纪城市风景建设与皇家园林艺术的最高水准。圆明园的声名远播西方，被誉为"万园之园"和"中国一切造园艺术的典范"。

　　圆明园是人工平地建造的大型水景园，其整体布局撷取传统士人园林"小中见大"的艺术手法，在掇山理水，塑造佳景胜境的同时，将中国古代构想的世界图式概括地予以再现。

　　宫廷区"九州清晏"，以后湖为构景中心，环湖九岛象征"禹贡九州"，寓意天下一统。

　　福海启创雍正（1723－1735年）初年，是园内最辽阔的水域。水中央筑"蓬岛瑶台"，比附传说中的蓬莱、方丈、瀛洲三仙山，福海即成为东海的化身。

园西北隅的"紫碧山房"积石成岭，为全园制高点，是西方昆仑神话的象征和写照。园内人工叠筑的丘壑山林以西山群峰为衬托，连绵起伏，宛然天然林壑的延续。穿流于山间、平原的曲涧清溪自西向东，漫流不息，将大小湖泊缀联成为一个丰富而完整的河湖水系。随峰回路转，水面开合，时而幽深宁静，时而开朗辽阔，创造出山外青山、绿水萦回、变化无尽的园林气氛，不是天然而胜似天然。

盛时圆明园有风景名胜、园中之园、宫殿寺庙百余处，荟萃了宫殿、园林、寺庙、村居、市肆等我国古代建筑的主要基本类型。建筑形式也几乎囊括了中国古代建筑可能出现的一切平面布局和造型式样，既有常见的单檐卷棚屋面，又有宫殿式重檐琉璃瓦顶；既有一进两厢、二进四厢的规整院落，又有灵活多变的园林建筑群组。建筑平面除常见的矩形、方形、圆形、工字、凸字、六角、八角外，更有十字、口字、田字、万字、曲尺、三角、方胜、偃月、扇面等罕见式样。为祭祀康熙、雍正而建的安佑宫布局严谨、气势恢宏，而仿自扬州的蒨园又亭台错落，宛转多姿……各式亭台楼阁与山形水体、花鸟树石穿插组合、相映成趣，构成一区区各具特色、丰富多彩的风景建筑群组，它们或隐现于山环水际之中，或突出于山巅水泊之外形成另一区主景，共同造就了圆明园特有的园中有园的集锦式园林风格。

圆明园的造景题材包罗万象，从政治说教到儒学经典，从宗教祈求到民间百态，天上人间，应有尽有。其中占绝对优势的是对传说中仙山楼阁的模拟，对古人诗情画意的再现和对自然山水、名胜古迹的概括提炼。"四十景"中，有取材于唐代大诗人李白"两水夹明镜，双桥落彩虹"诗意的"夹镜鸣琴"；有再现东晋陶渊明《桃花源记》描述的世外桃源的"武陵春色"；有融汇晚唐诗人杜牧《清明》诗意成景的"杏花春馆"；还有表现宋人范仲淹《岳阳楼记》所描述的洞庭湖岳阳楼气势的"上下天光"……"蓬岛瑶台"仿唐代画家李思训首创的金碧山水画意，仿佛"金堂五所，玉楼十二"；长春园"海岳开襟"，水中石砌汉白玉圆台之上，三重檐琉璃瓦层楼横空而起，远望缥渺如海市蜃楼，近临恍若仙界。其它还有"北远山村"，取意王维田家诗，寓意重农；"坐石临流"祖述绍兴兰亭，附庸风雅；"买卖街"嘈杂全如闹市；而"月地云居"梵呗声声，又宛然清净佛土。种种奇观胜景，不一而足，圆明园无愧名副其实的万园之园。

乾隆六下江南，凡所中意的名园胜景，皆命随行画师绘成范本，归而仿建御园之中。最著名的，有杭州西湖十景，连名称也一一沿用。长春园中的"如园"、"鉴园"、"狮子林"、"小有天园"分别曲肖南京瞻园、扬州趣园、苏州狮子林和杭州壑庵。圆明园"四宜书屋"规仿海宁安澜园，也易名为"安澜园"。这些园中之园在摄取原型神韵的同时，有取舍地进行因地制宜的再创作，把北国皇家园林的造园艺术推向一个新的高度。此外，从1747年到1783年，还由欧洲传教士郎世宁（Giuseppe GASTIGLLONE 1688 – 1766 意大利人）、蒋友仁（Michel BENOIT 1743 – 1774 法国人）、王致诚（Jean-Denis ATTLRET 1702 – 1768 法国人）等人负责设计，在长春园北部陆续建成一区欧式宫殿和喷泉，俗称"西洋楼"。中国园林史上，如此大规模地引进西方园林建筑尚属首例，是东西方文化与建筑交流史上引人注目的一页。

圆明园中花木繁茂，依景象的季相交替创造出不同的环境气氛，以植物著称而成景的有"牡丹台"、"桃花坞"、"芰荷香"、"君子轩"、"深柳读书堂"多处，江南的梅花、西洋的含羞草也在园中培植生根。在繁茂的绿阴花海中，更豢养有无数珍禽：白猿、麋鹿、仙鹤、孔雀、天鹅乃至池中的五色金鲤，无不是园景的有机组成部分。盛时圆明园何啻一座18、19世纪皇家动物园和植物园。

圆明园又是当时全国最重要的皇家博物馆和图书馆。在装修精美、陈设富丽的宫殿以及专用库房中，陈列、收藏有历代图籍重宝、名画书法，汇同玉器、名瓷、青铜、珐琅、钟表等来自全国与世界各地的希世奇珍；更遑论充斥其间、难以胜计的金银珠翠、绮缎织绣、衣冠服饰与家具文玩。

乾隆年间编纂的当时世界上最大的丛书——《四库全书》和《四库全书荟要》之一部，就分别贮藏于圆明园文源阁与长春园味腴书室。长春园淳化轩两廊镶嵌乾隆《钦定重刻淳化阁帖》，刻工精到，不亚于北海阅古楼《三希堂法帖》。舍卫城中，收贮数万尊金、银、铜佛以及金塔、金曼达和经卷，堪称佛教艺术宝库。

圆明园凝聚了无数能工哲匠的聪明智慧，是中华民族古老文明的象征和缩影。

道光（1821－1850年）以降，社会危机日益严重，清政府财力日拙。但道光皇帝宁撤"三山"陈设，罢木兰"秋狝"，仍不遗余力地对圆明园经营维护。虽已远不能与乾、嘉时代相比，但每年仅岁修费也超过白银十万两。直至园毁前夕，咸丰皇帝仍有"清晖堂"等土木兴作，圆明园居于当时政治中心的重要地位与清帝对它的珍视可想而知。

1856年，第二次鸦片战争爆发。清政府忽战忽和，屡失时机，最终在英法联军进逼下节节败退。1860年9月，咸丰逃往热河。10月，英法联军劫掠、火烧圆明园。数日之内，几世积存于园中的文物、珍宝被抢劫、毁损殆尽，一代名园惨遭焚毁。成为中国，也是世界近代文明史上的一场浩劫。

同治年间（1862－1874年），慈禧太后曾计划部分修复圆明园，但终因财力枯竭，半途而废。

1900年，八国联军侵华，京畿大乱。圆明园劫余幸存的少量建筑与古树名木遭到彻底毁灭。随着清王朝的覆亡，遗址上的石雕、奇石、砖瓦又被大量盗卖、取用，黍离麦秀，昔日的"万园之园"渐同荒野，一代名园的盛衰兴亡从一个侧面反映了清王朝由盛而衰而亡的历史。

今天，圆明园遗址已演化成为一部中国近代史的象征。湖光林影间，昔日的繁华富丽不复可寻，空余西洋楼数处孤零零的断垣残柱供人凭吊。苍烟落照，秋风春雨，予人以丰富而广阔的想像空间。"沉舟侧畔千帆过"，今日圆明园以其独具的悲剧美和历史感，唤起人们去追忆、去探求一个民族的盛衰治乱，它所蕴含的撼人心魄的力量与其特殊的历史地位，已远超出一座帝王山水宫苑遗址的本身。

1. Justness and Honesty
2. Clear Sky over Nine Prefectures
3. Front Lake
4. Rear Lake
5. Mountain High, River Long
6. Largeness of Mind
7. Peace and Harmony Everywhere
8. House of Apricot Blossoms in Spring
9. Light of the Sky High and Low
10. Lotus in the Breeze in a Curved Pond
11. Market Street
12. Garden of Shared Joy
13. Stone Seat by a Stream
14. Simplicity and Tranquility
15. Spring at Wuling
16. Moonlit Dwelling in Cloud
17. Sound of Oriole in Swaying Willows
18. Graceful Water and Trees
19. Buddha's City
20. Clear and Universal Justice
21. Elegance of the Western Peaks
22. Cloud-like Crops
23. Palace of Peace and Blessing
24. Purple and Green Mountain Lodge
25. Fish Jump and Kites Fly
26. Distant Northern Mountain Village
27. Taoist Wonderland
28. Lake of Blessing
29. Three Pools Reflecting the Moon
30. Garden of Gentle Ripples
31. Gentleman's Study
32. Sunset over Snowy Peaks
33. Ripples-Watching Hall
34. Land of Unique Beauty
35. Palace of Extensive Cultivation
36. Sound of Lute on Stream-Flanked Lake
37. Jasper Terrace on Penglai Island
38. Overlooking the Island of Immortals
39. Garden of Luxuriance
40. Vast Vistas of Sea and Mountains
41. Scripture-Storing Hall
42. Purifying Study
43. Likeness Garden
44. Mirror Garden
45. East Gate
46. Lion Wood
47. Baoxiang Temple
48. Building of Exotic Delights
49. Water Tower
50. Bird Cage
51. Labyrinth
52. Temple of Another Land
53. Overseas Hall
54. House of a Distant Land
55. Great Fountain
56. Display Fountain
57. Parallel Mounds
58. Square River
59. Study of Four Accords
60. Phoenix and Unicorn Islet
61. Green-Mirroring Pavilion
62. Gate to the Garden of Beautiful Spring

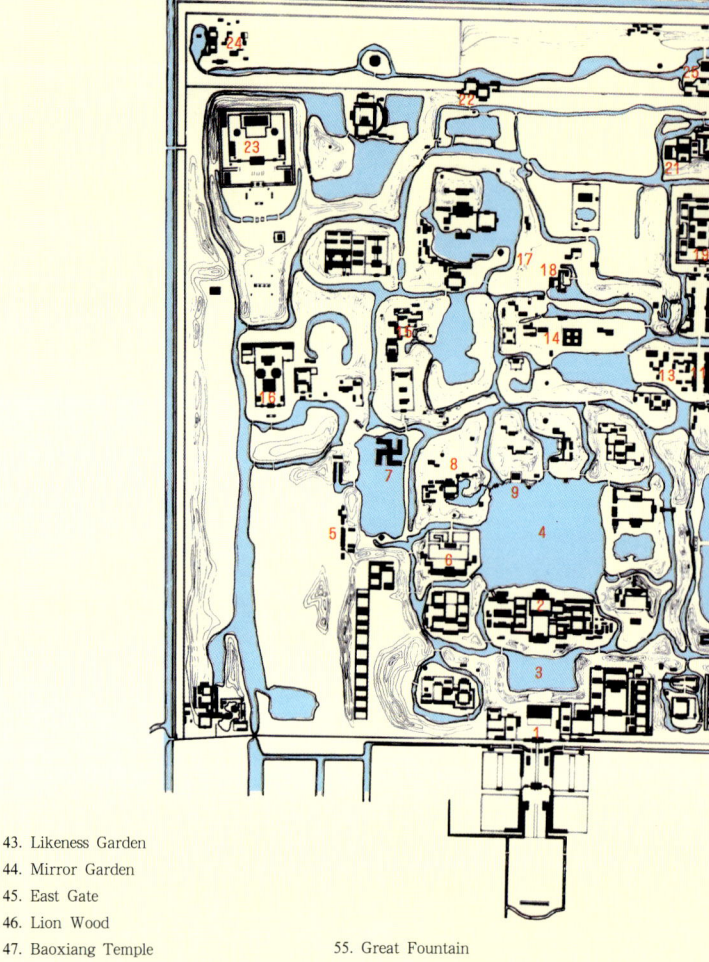

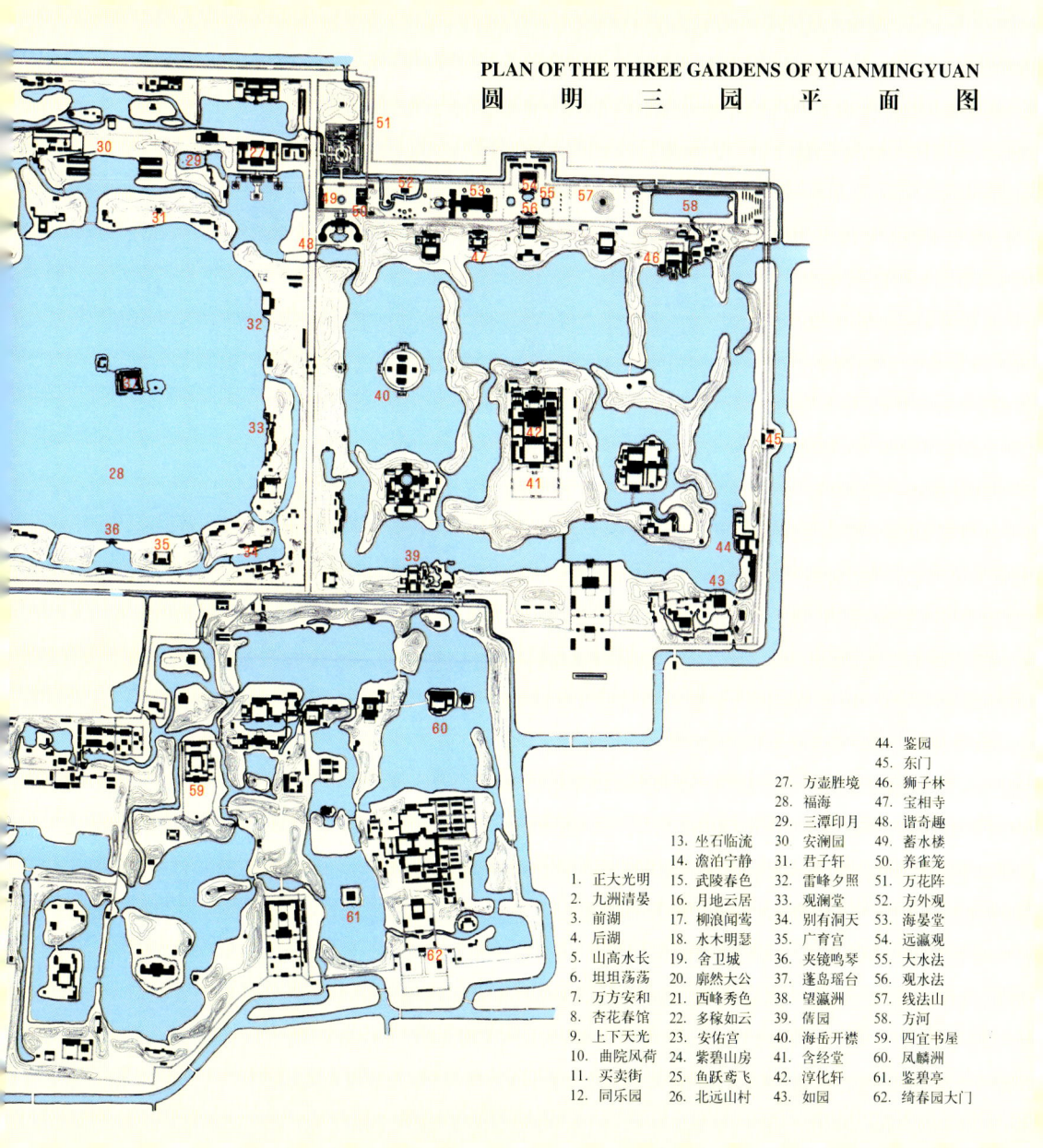

PLAN OF THE THREE GARDENS OF YUANMINGYUAN
圆明三园平面图

1. 正大光明
2. 九洲清晏
3. 前湖
4. 后湖
5. 山高水长
6. 坦坦荡荡
7. 万方安和
8. 杏花春馆
9. 上下天光
10. 曲院风荷
11. 买卖街
12. 同乐园
13. 坐石临流
14. 澹泊宁静
15. 武陵春色
16. 月地云居
17. 柳浪闻莺
18. 水木明瑟
19. 舍卫城
20. 廓然大公
21. 西峰秀色
22. 多稼如云
23. 安佑宫
24. 紫碧山房
25. 鱼跃鸢飞
26. 北远山村
27. 方壶胜境
28. 福海
29. 三潭印月
30. 安澜园
31. 君子轩
32. 雷峰夕照
33. 观澜堂
34. 别有洞天
35. 广育宫
36. 夹镜鸣琴
37. 蓬岛瑶台
38. 望瀛洲
39. 倩园
40. 海岳开襟
41. 含经堂
42. 淳化轩
43. 如园
44. 鉴园
45. 东门
46. 狮子林
47. 宝相寺
48. 谐奇趣
49. 蓄水楼
50. 养雀笼
51. 万花阵
52. 方外观
53. 海晏堂
54. 远瀛观
55. 大水法
56. 观水法
57. 线法山
58. 方河
59. 四宜书屋
60. 凤麟洲
61. 鉴碧亭
62. 绮春园大门

"Justness and Honesty"
This was originally the main hall in the Garden of Perfection and Enlightenment, where the Qing emperors held court. The inscribed board was in the hand of Emperor Yongzheng. There were sword-like rocks and ancient pines on the Hill of Long Life behind the solemn and quiet hall. The sword-like rocks have been moved to the path leading to Hanxin Pavilion at the foot of the Longevity Hill in the Summer Palace.

"正大光明"
原为圆明园正殿,雍正题额,是清帝视朝之所。殿后寿山剑石壁立,古松苍然,景象清幽肃穆。今颐和园万寿山麓含新亭山径边的剑石即为寿山遗物。

Notes: 1) The names within quotation marks are the names given to the scenic spots in Yuanmingyuan in the Qing dynasty.

2) The pictures of Yuanmingyuan reproduced in this book were the works of court painters of the Qing dynasty. They are preserved in museums in China and abroad.

注：①凡图片标题加引号者，为清代时圆明园景区名称，下文同。

②书中圆明园景区绘画均为清代宫廷画师所作，现藏于海内外博物馆。

A portrait of Emperor Qianlong by Guiseppe Castiglione.
Qianlong was the longest ruling emperor of China of all time. Dressed in everyday clothes and looking serene and dignified, he is presented here as both an emperor and a man of letters.

乾隆皇帝画像（郎世宁绘）
乾隆是统治中国时间最长的君主。画中皇帝身穿常服，神态庄重安详，正是帝王兼文人双重身分的写照。

"Clear Sky over Nine Prefectures."
This was the sleeping palace of the Qing emperors. With a lake in front and behind it, this was an extension of the palace area and the beginning of the scenic area. The nine islets in the Rear Lake were built during the reign of Emperor Yongzheng. They set the standard for the size of the landscapes in Yuanmingyuan. Structures built or expanded later in the garden were all based on the size of the islets.

"九州清晏"
是清帝的寝宫，前后临湖。既是宫廷区的延续，又是苑景区的起始。后湖九岛雍正年间即已建成，它们奠定了圆明园山水布局的尺度。以后御园的增修、扩建，均以此为基础而进行。

"Mountain High, River Long"

Known as the "Audience Hall" in Emperor Yongzheng's time, this was the place for giving banquets to envoys from vassal states and for the guards to practise archery. The storeyed building of nine bays without elaborate ornaments had an open space in front, which afforded a broad vista. A banquet was held here every year at the Lantern Festival together with grand fireworks display during the reigns of Emperors Qianlong and Jiaqing.

"山高水长"

雍正时称"引见楼",是外藩朝正赐宴和侍卫日常练射处。重楼九间,朴素无华,前临平川,视野开阔。乾隆、嘉庆朝历年元宵节均在此设灯宴、举行盛大的烟火晚会。

Lake of Blessing

Lovely scenery was to be found on every one of the 10 islets around the Lake of Blessing designed in the same way as that of the Rear Lake, but wider in scope. There were coves on the edge of the lake, where scenic sights and small gardens were linked together with those on the lake to echo one another and form a contrast between open vistas and seclusion.

福海

福海四周十岛环绕,佳景云集,与后湖的造景手法如出一辙,只是更加辽阔。外侧曲港回转,贯串数处景点和小园,与福海隔而不断,若即若离,互为因借,形成开朗与幽深的对比。

"Jasper Terrace on Penglai Island"

This scenic sight was formed by the "Jasper Terrace on Penglai Island," "Immortals Mountain on the Sea" and another building at the centre of the Lake of Blessing, based on the traditional layout of "one lake and three mountains" in imperial gardens. The gate structure, known as "Pavilion in the Mirror" was exotically structured. The main hall, the "Spring Retaining Hall," was furnished with a jade screen and other precious objects. The "Mind-Opening Tower" in the east and the platform in the west offered distant views. At Qianlong's time, the Empress Dowager was invited here every year at the Dragon Boat Festival to watch the dragon boat race.

"蓬岛瑶台"

位于福海中心,由"蓬岛瑶台"、"瀛海仙山"等三组建筑组成,为中国皇家园林"一池三山"的传统模式。门殿"镜中阁"造型奇丽,正宇"留春殿"内有玉屏风等珍贵陈设。东部"畅襟楼"和西部平台可供登临远眺,乾隆时历年端午节于此迎奉皇太后观龙舟竞渡。

17

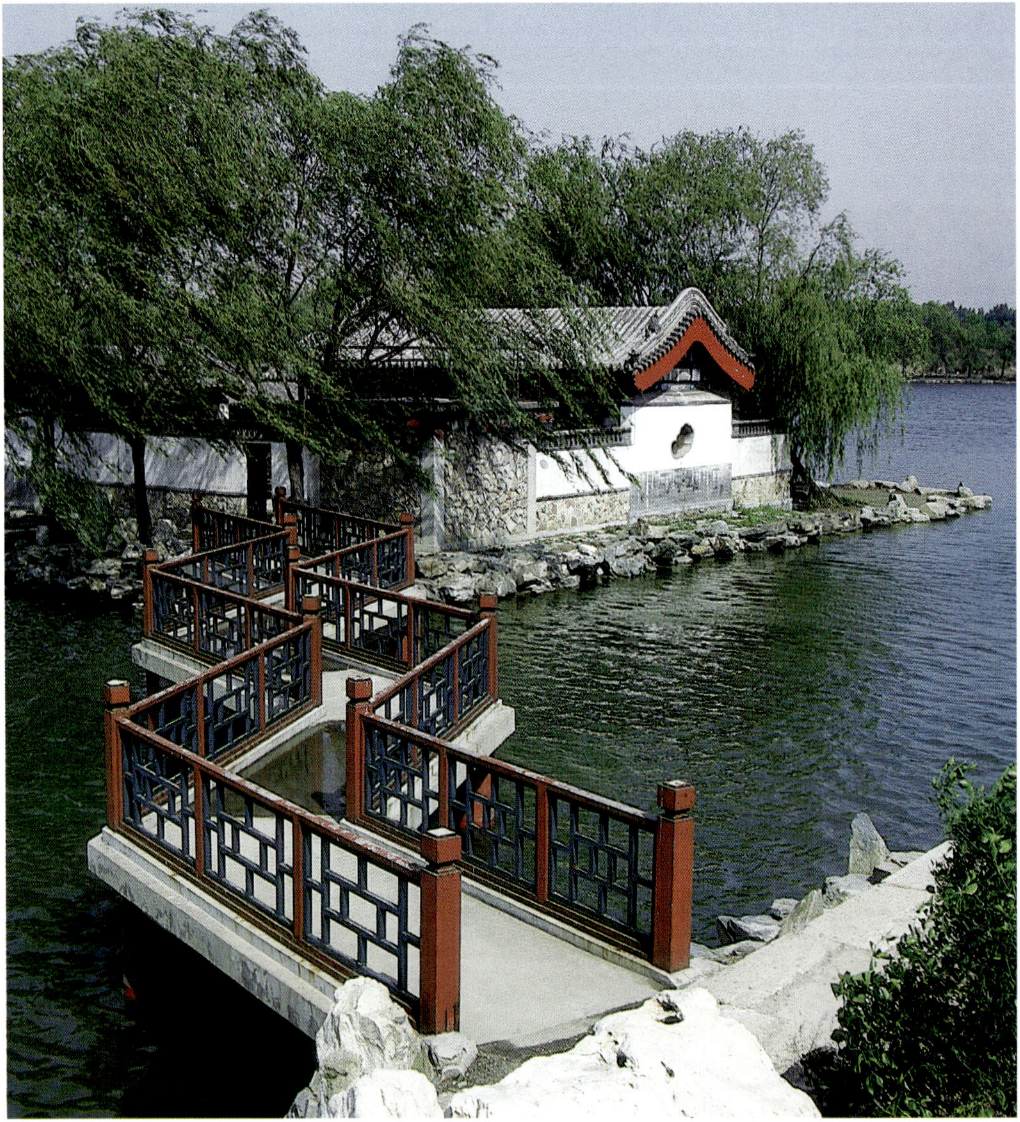

Ice on the lake begins to melt in spring.
冬去春来

Morning at the Five-Arch Bridge on the Lake of Blessing.
福海五孔桥晨曲

◀ A courtyard on a western islet in the Lake of Blessing.
福海西岛庭院

19

The newly built Jade-Ribbon Bridge stands where the Lake of Blessing joins the surrounding river system.
新建于福海与四周水系交汇处的玉带桥

Yuanmingyuan is still a good place to go for a day of leisure.
今天的圆明园仍然是人们休息、娱乐的好去处。

22

"Simplicity and Tranquility"

This area was popularly known as the "Four-Square House" with paddy fields and reeds nearby. Together with "Reflections in Water of Fragrant Orchid," it formed a pastoral scene to express the theme of attaching importance to farming.

"澹泊宁静"

俗称"田字房"。附近水田数顷，蒲苇瑟瑟，与"映水兰香"共同组成一区以重农为主题思想的园林景观。

"Peace and Harmony Everywhere"

Built in the fifth year of Emperor Yongzheng (1727), this was one of the most characteristic garden structures in Yuanmingyuan. The waterside pavilions of 33 rooms were linked and extended to the centre of the lake. As it was warm in winter and cool in summer, this garden was much favoured by Emperor Yongzheng.

"万方安和"

建于雍正五年（1727），是圆明园最具特色的园林建筑之一。33间水榭彼此相连，宛转池心，冬暖而夏凉，雍正最喜居此。

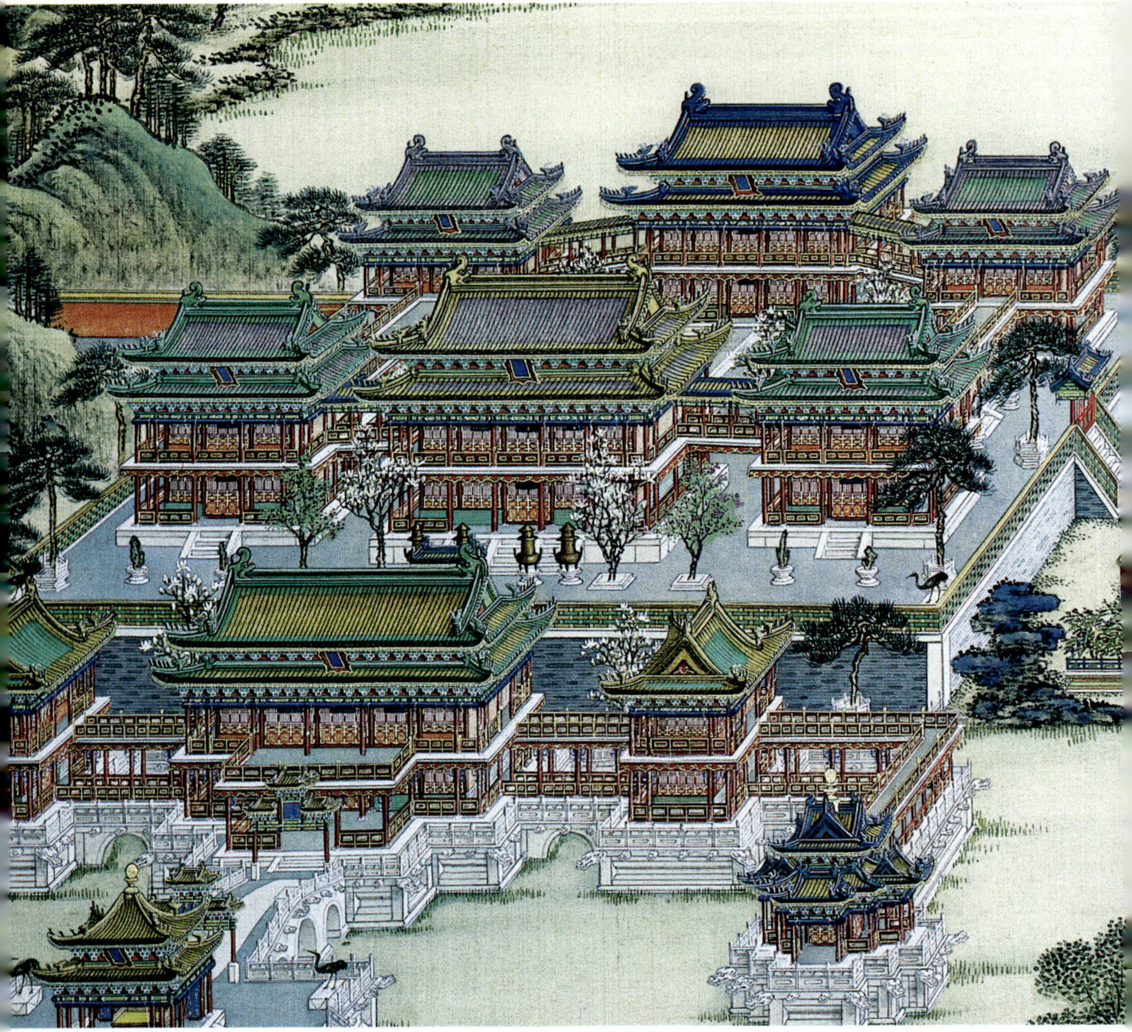

◀ **"Taoist Wonderland"**

The principal architectural style of Yuanmingyuan was one that emphasized seclusion and gracefulness, dignity and splendour. The "Taoist Wonderland" was a large complex of palace buildings erected in the first year of Emperor Qianlong (1736). All the structures in the complex were symmetrically arranged and covered with glazed roof tiles like the resplendent dwelling of Taoist immortals.

"方壶胜境"

圆明园的主体风格,一是幽深婉约,一是端庄华贵。"方壶胜境"是乾隆初年(1736)经营的大型宫殿群组之一,整体成对称布局,全部覆以琉璃瓦,金碧辉煌,巍若仙居。

Ruins of the "Taoist Wonderland."
"方壶胜境"遗址

Ruins of the "Ripples-Watching Hall"

"Watching ripples" comes from Mencius, who said, "It requires skill to see how the water flows; one must watch its ripples." The names of many of the buildings in the three gardens of Yuanmingyuan, while describing scenery, had political connotations, such as "Tolerance and Clear Seeing" and "Gentleman's Study." This practice was a special feature in naming the scenic sights in Chinese classical gardens. The Ripples-Watching Hall was a large building of five bays wide with a three-ridged roof and surrounded by corridors. It faced the lake and the "Jasper Terrace on Penglai Island" on the opposite shore. The western side offered the best view of the Western Hills. At dusk, when the hills and trees were reflected in the lake and when rosy clouds constantly changed shapes, the scenery was majestic. The hall was built in the 22nd year of Emperor Jiaqing (1817) on the foundations of a group of pavilions south of the "Mountain Lodge of Joint Elegance." This reconstruction showed that the scenic structures in the garden changed continually and could not be wholly covered by the 40 scenic sights.

观澜堂遗址

"观澜"语出孟子"观水有术，必观其澜"。圆明三园中许多园林建筑的命名皆为写景的同时暗喻为政，如"涵虚朗鉴""君子轩"等，这也是中国古典园林景题命名的特色之一。观澜堂体量庞大，五间三卷周围以廊。俯临一湖碧水，与"蓬岛瑶台"相顾盼，西望可借景西山，景色最佳。黄昏时分，层峰倒影，云霞顷刻变幻，气象万千。此堂是嘉庆22年（1817）在"接秀山房"偏南的一组亭榭基础上改建而成。由此可见，园中景物变迁日新月异，已非四十景图所能概括。

Palace of Peace and Blessing
Built in the eighth year of Emperor Qianlong (1743), this palace was structured in the same way as the Imperial Ancestral Temple.

安佑宫
建成于乾隆八年（1743），制同太庙。

"Sound of Lute on Stream-Flanked Lake"
There is a scenic sight named "A Mirror-like Lake Flanked by Two Ponds" at the Imperial Summer Resort in Chengde. "Sound of Lute on Stream-Flanked Lake" in Yuanmingyuan with music in the name was more poetic and picturesque.

"夹镜鸣琴"
避暑山庄有"双湖夹镜"一景。圆明园"夹镜鸣琴"以声入景，更富诗情画意。

"Spring at Wuling"(detail)

This was one of the earliest scenic areas built in Yuanmingyuan. The hillocks and streams were interspersed with thousands of peach trees. When the petals fell in late spring, it presented a picture of the Land of Peach Blossoms with luxuriant grass and colourful fallen flowers. Picture shows the Peach Blossom Cave.

"武陵春色"（局部）

是圆明园最早建成的景区之一，山重水复，桃花万株。春深花落，正是桃花源"芳草鲜美，落英缤纷"的景象写照。画中为桃花洞。

Ruins of "Spring at Wuling."
"武陵春色"遗址

"Light of the Sky High and Low."
"上下天光"

"House of Apricot Blossoms in Spring"

This was called "Vegetable Garden" in Emperor Yongzheng's time. There were the "Apricot Blossom Village" and other small structures here. The "Pavilion of Spring Rain" was added in the 20th year of Emperor Qianlong, where the Qing emperors often came to watch the rain falling on apricot flowers in spring. The name described the mood of a famous line in one of Du Mu's poems: "The rain drizzles down at the Clear and Bright Festival."

"杏花春馆"

雍正时称"菜圃",有"杏花村"等小建筑。乾隆二十年(1755)增建"春雨轩",清帝常于此观雨。于时杏花盛开,春雨蒙蒙,杜牧名句"清明时节雨纷纷"的意境自出。

"Distant Northern Mountain Village."
There was a narrow strip of land of 1,600 metres from east to west and about 100 metres wide in the northern part of Yuanmingyuan. The builders cleverly partitioned it with lotus ponds, paddy fields, vegetable plots, orchards and hillocks and enlivened it with a stream running through it. The low buildings, fences, pavilions and terraces on both banks transformed it into a picturesque place like the land of rivers and lakes in the south.

"北远山村"
圆明园北部有一东西长约1600米、南北仅百余米的狭长地带。造园者以荷塘、稻田、菜畦、果园和山岭巧妙分隔,又以一水纵贯,点活全局。两岸或矮屋疏篱,或楼台掩映,风光绮丽明媚,宛然江南水乡。

"Fish Jump, Kites Fly"
The huge storeyed main building spanned a stream and was the principal structure in the northern part of Yuanmingyuan. The top storey offered a view of the surrounding pastoral scenery.

"鱼跃鸢飞"
巨大的主楼横跨水面,为圆明园北区风水之镇。登楼四望,一派田园风光。

Market Street

The Market Street in this picture is crowded with shops. It was said that when the emperor came here, eunuchs masqueraded as vendors. To the north of the Market Street was the "Buddha's City" and to the east, the "Garden of Shared Joy," where there was a three-storeyed theatrical stage. On New Year's Day, the emperor's birthday and other festival days, the emperor invited the Empress Dowager, nobles and ministers over to enjoy an opera performance. Hidden in the hillocks to the west was the famous "Orchid Pavilion," where a clear spring flew over white stones and through green vegetation and formed a sharp contrast against the noisy Market Street and between activities and quietude.

Ruins of the walls of Buddha's City
舍卫城城墙遗址

买卖街

图中绘店铺林立的买卖街。相传当年帝后临幸这里时，由太监充任商贩。街北即"舍卫城"，街东为"同乐园"，园中有三层大戏台，每年元旦、万寿等节日，皇帝迎奉太后，率王公、贵臣在此听戏。街西山怀中即著名的"兰亭"，白石清泉，碧萝萦带，与背后喧闹的街市恰成动与静的鲜明对比。

This three-storeyed theatrical stage in the Garden of Virtue and Harmony in the Summer Palace, built during the reign of Emperor Guangxu (1875-1908), is a copy of the stage in the "Garden of Shared Joy" It attests to the former grandeur of Yuanmingyuan.

今颐和园德和园三层大戏台,是光绪年间(1875 – 1908年)依 "同乐园" 戏台修建的,由此可想见圆明园当时盛况。

"Moonlit Dwelling in Cloud"

Emperor Qianlong was a Buddhist and pretended himself to be Bodhisattva Manjusri. He encouraged the Yellow Sect to win over the upper strata of the Tibetans and Mongolians and closely observed the Buddhist religious rules himself. The "Pure Land" was the most important temple of Tibetan Buddhism in the imperial garden. "Moonlit Dwelling in Cloud," the main hall of the temple built in the traditional style of lamaist temples in the Tibet area, was a multi-eaved square structure of five bays wide and deep, different from the Buddhist temples in the Han area. Its red walls and gray roof tiles half hidden behind green pines created a solemn and serene atmosphere.

"月地云居"

乾隆笃信佛教，以文殊自许。在兴黄教，安抚西藏、蒙古上层人士的同时，自己也身体力行。"清净地"就是御园中最重要的一处藏传佛教寺院。正殿"月地云居"采用青海、西藏地区喇嘛寺常见的"都罡法式"，为一面阔、进深各五间的重檐方亭，有异于汉地佛寺。红墙灰瓦，青松掩映，庄严静穆。

"Traces of Snow on a Broken Bridge" at the upper left corner of the picture depicts a scene similar to a famous sight at Hangzhou's West Lake. The pavilion at the lower right corner is named "Looking for the Ferry." In the pavilion are two inscribed lines from Tao Yuanming in the hand of Emperor Qianlong: "Clouds flow out of the mountains not by themselves; Tired birds know when it is time to go home." They foretell his intention to abdicate and spend his time in care-free leisure after 60 years on the throne.

画中左上角为"断桥残雪",写仿杭州西湖同名风景又不尽相似。右下角山石间敞厅名"问津",内挂乾隆御书陶渊明句:"云无心以出岫,鸟倦飞而知还。"预示他日后做满60年天子当禅位,优游林下。

Ruins of "Traces of Snow on a Broken Bridge."
"断桥残雪"遗迹

"Lotus in the Breeze in a Curved Pond"
Most of the copies of the 10 scenic sights of the West Lake in Yuanmingyuan were far different from their originals. Some were unsuccessful imitations. But "Lotus in the Breeze in a Curved Pond" was distinctive in style when lotus flowers blossomed in the pond in the summer. The pond was echoed by the nine-arch bridge in the south of the pond.

"曲院风荷"
圆明园中的所谓西湖十景，多与原型相去甚远，有的也并不成功。但"曲院风荷"夏日荷花满池，风格独特。池南以九孔桥横卧波心，与其相呼应。

Site of the nine-arch bridge and the pond.
九孔桥及水池遗址

37

"Leifeng Pagoda in the Setting Sun"
The scenic sight from this spot on the eastern shore of the Lake of Blessing with the pagoda on the Hill of Jade Spring, Tower of Buddhist Fragrance on the Hill of Longevity and the Western Hills in the background was a successful copy of the 10 scenic sights of the West Lake.

"雷峰夕照"
地处福海东岸,借景玉泉山宝塔、万寿山佛香阁以及西山群峰,是御园摹仿西湖十景较为成功的一处。

Sunset on the Lake of Blessing from the spot of "Leifeng Pagoda in the Setting Sun."
"雷峰夕照"处看福海夕阳

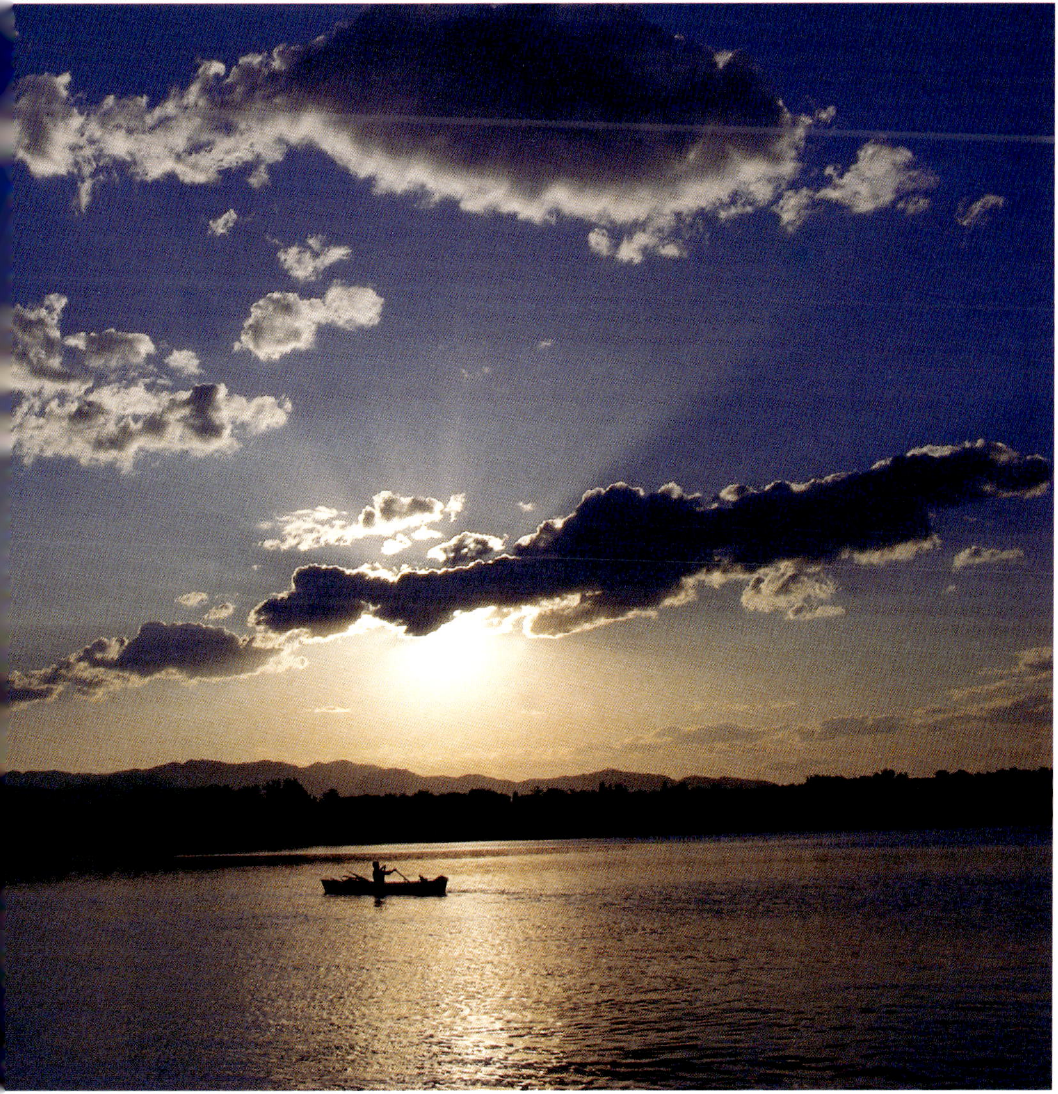

"Elegance of the Western Peaks"
Emperor Yongzheng was well versed in Buddhism. "Elegance of the Western Peaks" was one of the earliest scenic sights created in Yuanmingyuan. With the Western Hills in the background, a waterfall on Mount Lushan was recreated here with rockery to represent the dwelling of Hui Yuan, a high monk in Eastern Jin time. Qianlong also compared the six magnolias in front of the Studio of Insinuating Rhythm to the "Six Care-free Men of the Bamboo Creek," including the poet Li Bai. The scenic sight created a variable mood by combining culture, history, famous mountain and famous site into one.

"西峰秀色"
雍正具有很深的佛学造诣。西峰秀色是圆明园最早建成的苑景之一。它以西山峰峦为底衬，人工叠石写意庐山瀑布，暗喻东晋高僧惠远在庐山的东林精舍。乾隆更将含韵斋前的六株玉兰比为李白等"竹溪六逸"，园林造景与人文历史、名山胜境融合于一体，意境丰富。

"Three Pools Reflecting the Moon"
West of the "Taoist Wonderland" and on the other side of the Bridge of Gushing Gold, this scenic sight of pavilions and rocks in the water was a modified copy of the scenic sight of the same name at West Lake. It looked rather confined and lacking in space.

"三潭印月"
在"方壶胜境"西边、过涌金桥、亭廊卧波、水石玲珑，为西湖同名风景的变体之作，幽闭有余而旷达不足。

Angling. 垂钓

Site of the "Sound of Oriole in Swaying Willows."
"柳浪闻莺"遗址

Spring breeze stirs again in Yuanmingyuan.
春风又吹圆明园

43

44

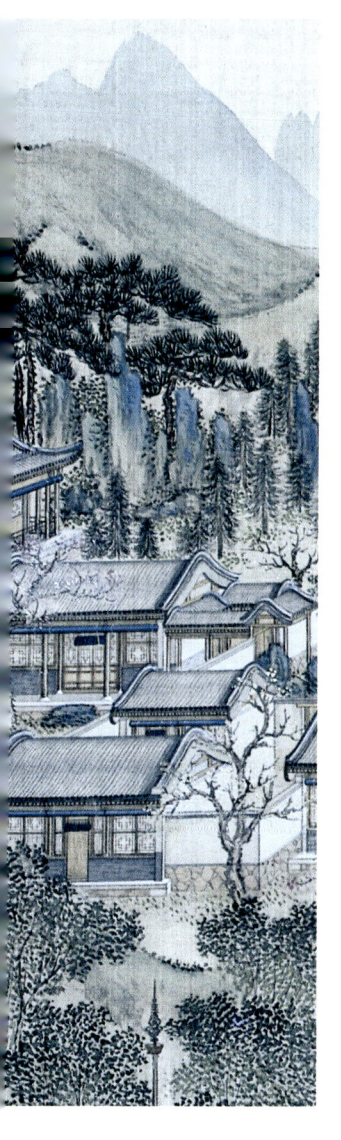

Ruins of "Clear and Universal Justice"

"Clear and Universal Justice" came from the philosopher Cheng Zi. There used to be a pair of cranes staying in the front yard. The building was, therefore, also called "Twin Cranes Studio." In the 20th year of Qianlong (1755), the area was rebuilt roughly on the patent of the Garden of Sustained Freedom in Wuxi and became a sister garden of the Huishan Garden in the Garden of Clear Ripples (the Garden of Harmonious Delights in the Summer Palace today).

"廓然大公"遗迹

"廓然大公"语出程子, 前庭常有一对仙鹤栖息, 因此也称"双鹤斋"。乾隆二十年 (1755), 仿无锡寄畅园大意重修, 与清漪园之惠山园 (今颐和园谐趣园) 并称双璧。

"Study of Four Accords"

This picture of the "Study of Four Accords" was painted in the ninth year of Qianlong (1744). Twenty years later, a copy of Chen's Garden of Gentle Ripples in Haining was built here with 10 scenic sights, such as the "Purity Tower in Misty Moonlight," "Pavilion of Boundless Wind and Moon," "Flower-Picking Islet," "Pavilion of Beautiful Glances" and "Green-Curtained Boat." The spot was then renamed "Garden of Gentle Ripples."

"四宜书屋"

画为乾隆九年 (1744) 的四宜书屋。20年后, 这里仿海宁陈氏安澜园建成"烟月清真楼"、"无边风月之阁""采芳洲""飞睇亭""绿帷舫"等十景, 易名"安澜园"。

"Land of Unique Beauty"

There were many small gardens on the edge of the Lake of Blessing, including the "Clear and Universal Justice" and "Land of Unique Beauty" respectively at the northwestern and southeastern corners. These gardens directly or indirectly imitated the structure and mood of famous gardens in the south and created a rich variety of beautiful tracts. The "Land of Unique Beauty," also known as the "Elegant Village" was hidden in a cove surrounded by hillocks and trees. Its serene beauty formed a contrast against the broad Lake of Blessing. Emperor Yongzheng once tried to make Taoist pills of immortality here. The garden was also frequented by Emperors Qianlong, Jaiqing and Daoguang.

"别有洞天"

福海外环多小园,"廓然大公"、"别有洞天"分处西北与东南角。它们或直接摹仿、或间接吸收江南名园的结构和意境,创造出丰富多变的园林空间。"别有洞天"也称"秀清村",位于一隐闭的水湾内,小山丛树环抱,清幽宁静,与福海的开阔恢宏恰成鲜明对比。雍正曾在此处开炉炼丹。乾隆、嘉庆、道光诸帝来这里游览、进膳。

A winding stream leading to seclusion.
曲溪通幽

西域貢貽威貧言毬掌尾非奇彌珠毛
翠角圍可啟掌邱成鏡單翠聞歲荷乃
青雨散紉翼之領圃屬貢憶崎
從志雀紱紑之邀三年小尾大花
下閒屏尾翠綠羽眼且圓眼凌
風張尾既然條高屆那爲寬代瑠
箒拾之卸末抦之年屋朝知窓知升
俞余點土產好教援脫人源亟廷濟
牧朱錐支 枝 捲児懋挹
戊寅六自艱堂
　　　御筆

◀ **A Peacock Unfurling Its Fan by Guiseppe Castiglione**

The two peacocks in this picture were hatched and raised in the imperial garden. They were tame and lovable, responded to calls and danced to the clapping of hands. Emperor Qianlong wrote a special poem and had it inscribed on the painting, which was originally in the Mountain Studio of Dense Bamboos and is now preserved in Taipei's Imperial Palace Museum.

郎世宁绘《孔雀开屏》

图中的两只孔雀是在御园孚育、长成的、驯服可爱，能招之即来并合拍起舞。乾隆特为此事赋诗并命词臣代笔书于其上。此图原存竹密山斋，今藏台北故宫。

White Monkeys painted by Guiseppe Castiglione.
郎世宁绘《白猿》

Spring at the "Land of Unique Beauty."
"别有洞天"春景

Peach Blossom Dock

This was an area of green pines and willows and pink peach blossoms north of "Spring at Wuling", where Emperor Qianlong lived and studied when he was young.

桃花坞

位于"武陵春色"北部，苍松偃盖，柳绿桃红，曾是乾隆皇帝少时园居读书处。

Fragrance of Lotus Flowers

This spot north of "Cloud-like Crops" was an ideal place for enjoying lotus flowers in the summer.

芰荷香

位于"多稼如云"处，是夏日赏荷胜地。

Willow-Hidden Study

Willow was one of the principal trees in Yuanmingyuan. The Willow-Hidden Study in the shade of old willow trees was on the western shore of the Lake of Blessing. The square pavilion on the southeastern shore was called "Overlooking the Island of Immortals," where Emperors Qianlong, Daoguang and Xianfeng used to watch dragon-boat races with their ministers at the Dragon-Boat Festival.

深柳读书堂

柳树是圆明园的主要植物之一。深柳读书堂掩映古柳浓阴中,地处福海西岸。其东南临湖的四方亭,名"望瀛洲",是乾隆、道光、咸丰端午节率臣下观龙舟竞渡的地方。

Site of the Palace of Extensive Cultivation.
广育宫遗址

◀ **"Graceful Water and Trees"**
This scenic area included the "Fishing Rock" and "Scale-Washing Pool," where crucian carp were bred for the kitchen. The Fan Room here, where the fan was worked by the Western hydraulic method, was a gadget that preceded the fountains at the Western Buildings. Emperor Yongzheng often came here to cool himself.

"水木明瑟"
包括"钓鱼矶"、"濯鳞沼"等景点，养育热河鲫鱼，以供烹饪。此地的风扇室"用泰西水法，引水入室中以转风扇"，开西洋楼水法的先声。雍正常于此纳凉。

54

Garden of Eternal Spring after the first snow.
长春园初雪

◀ **Garden of Eternal Spring**

Construction of the Garden of Eternal Spring started in the ninth year of Qianlong (1744) and was basically completed in the 16th year (1751). It patterned on the scenery in the region of rivers and lakes in the south while drawing on the best of imperial and private gardens. After completion, it was renovated several times. There were more than 20 palace buildings, gardens and scenic sights positioned side by side on the hillocks and islets and by the lakes and streams. The imposing palace buildings, white-washed walls and deep courtyards formed a garden of natural and dignified style that conformed with the overall style of Yuanmingyuan but had its own distinctive features.

长春园

长春园始建于乾隆九年(1744),十六年(1751)初步完成。它以江南水国为蓝本,兼取皇家、私家园林之长,一次性规划、一次性施工,又渐次修改完善。园内有宫殿、园林、景点20余处,交错分布于山林岛屿上,湖泽溪河间,随水体的交换、山脉的延伸,时而琳宫巍峨,琼楼高起,时又粉垣环护,庭院深深,形成与圆明园既相统一又别具特色的平远自如、端庄华贵的园林风格。

Garden of Eternal Spring in the dusk.
长春园暮色

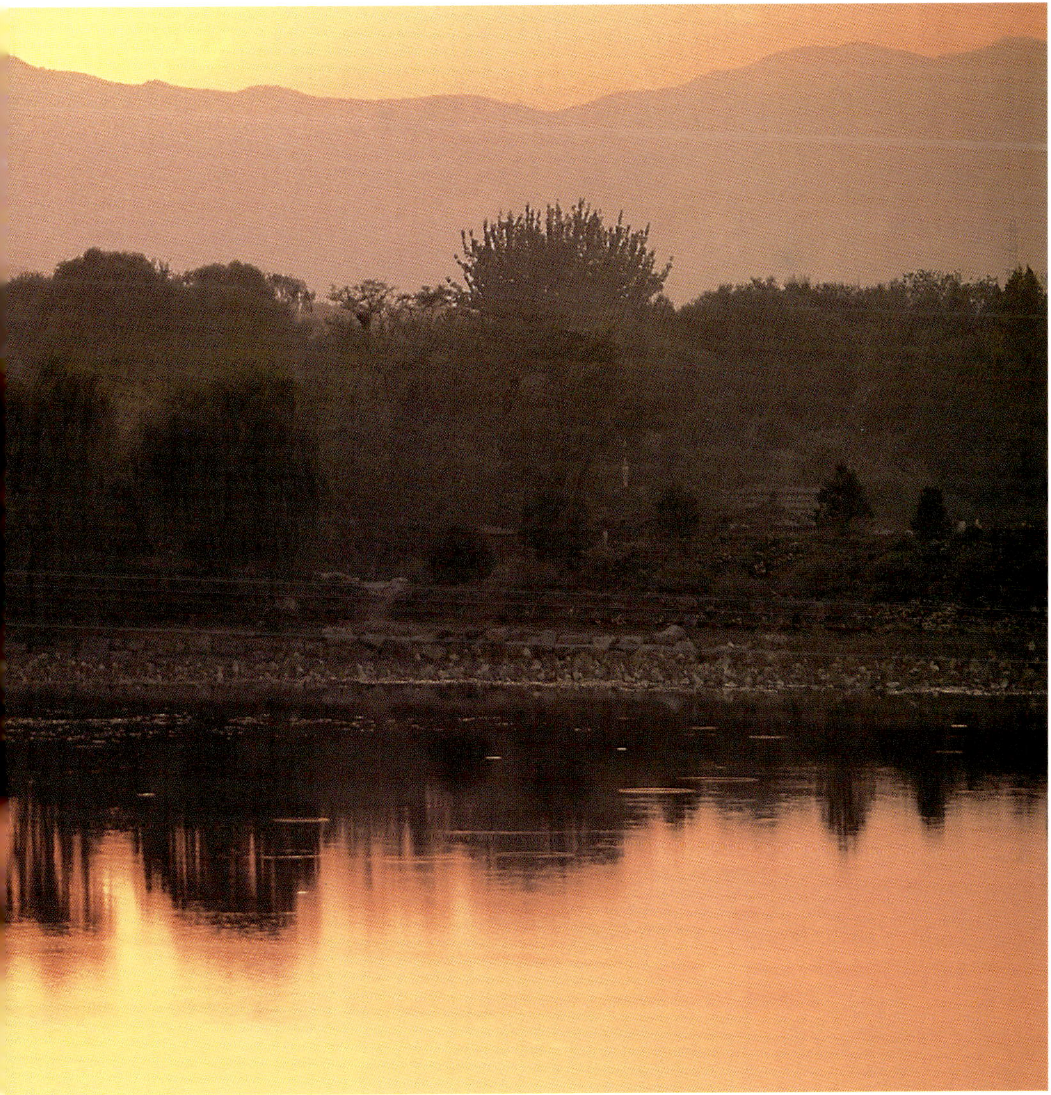

Ruins of the Scripture-Storing Hall and Purifying Study

The Scripture-Storing Hall at the centre of the islet in the Garden of Eternal Spring was a majestic structure like a palace in style. It covered 45,000 square metres of grounds and was completed at the same time as the garden. In 1770, Emperor Qianlong had it expanded and the Purifying Study added so that he could live in it as the emperor's father after he passed the throne to his son. Another Purifying Study of the same style was built in the Palace of Peace and Longevity in the Forbidden City.

含经堂、淳化轩遗址

中宫位于长春园中心岛上，与该园同期建成，总面积达45,000平方米，壮丽谨严，完全是皇宫气派。1770年，乾隆再次扩建，增修淳化轩等建筑，完成了他在御园中的太上皇宫殿，并将淳化轩一式二份地仿建于紫禁城宁寿宫。

Remains of the Plinth of a Column at the Purifying Study

The plinth of the column measures 1.20 × 1.20 metres. It has been deduced that the column should have been 0.6 metre in diameter, which is a rare size in the three gardens of Yuanmingyuan.

淳化轩柱础残迹

淳化轩遗存经柱柱础1.20 × 1.20米，推测其柱径应在0.60米左右，这在圆明三园中实属罕见。

This bronze dragon that used to stand in front of the Scripture-Storing Hall is now in the Fontainebleau Palace of Paris, France.

原摆放于含经堂宫门前的铜龙，今藏法国巴黎枫丹白露宫。

Site of the Mirror Garden

The Mirror Garden, an approximate copy of the Garden of Delight in Yangzhou, was located at the southeastern bend of the Long River around the Garden of Eternal Spring. It faced across the river the Likeness Garden, a copy of the Zhan Garden in Nanjing. With its waterside corridor overlooking the lake on the outside and the fish pond on the inside, it recreated the mood of the "Four Bridges in a Misty Rain" at the Spring Water Corridor and Half-a-Mu Pond at the Slender West Lake in Yangzhou.

鉴园遗址

鉴园规仿扬州"趣园"大意，地处长春园外围长河东南拐角，与肖仿南京"瞻园"的如园隔水相望。其水廊外瞰长湖清漪，内临鱼池，大有扬州瘦西湖"四桥烟雨"春水廊、半亩塘的意趣。

A poem in the hand of Emperor Jiaqing carved on the Pine-Supporting Rock in the Likeness Garden.

如园"称松岩"嘉庆御笔诗刻。

Lion Wood.
狮子林

Lion Wood

The Lion Wood, a famous garden in Suzhou, was originally the garden of a temple. The Lion Wood in the Garden of Eternal Spring was built in the 37th year of Qianlong (1772) with water in front and a hill behind and with spring water diverted into the lake along stepped stones. In emphasizing both seclusion and openness, it was even better than the Lion Wood in Suzhou. Qing emperors used to cruise in a boat through the water gate into the quiet garden with pavilions and terraces of different heights in it. Picture the foundation stones of Lion wood.

狮子林

苏州名园狮子林的前身是一处寺庙园林。长春园狮子林建于乾隆三十七年(1772),倚山面水,叠石引泉,奥旷两宜,较苏州狮子林更胜一筹。当年清帝常由开阔的湖面乘舟由水关进入亭台参错、幽深宁谧的小园。图为狮子林临水基石。

Remains of the water gate.
水门遗迹

Site of the "Vast Vistas of Sea and Mountains"
This was the finest and most spectacular of the scenic sights in the three gardens of Yuanmingyuan. The islet built of stone was shaped like a datura. The three-storeyed main building was flanked by symmetrically arranged multi-eaved side buildings and a square pavilion, circular corridors and arches with pines and rockery between them. It was like a fairyland on earth. It escaped destruction in 1860 and was visited by Empress Dowager Cixi and Emperor Guangxu. In 1900, it was destroyed by the scum of the nation.

"海岳开襟" 遗址
是圆明三园最精美奇特的园林景观。水中石砌圆岛成曼陀罗格局，主楼三层居中，有重檐配殿、重檐方亭、圆式游廊及牌坊对称环列，间以青松、奇石，宛若人间仙境。此地1860年幸免于难，慈禧太后曾携光绪来此游赏。1900年毁于民族败类之手。

Ruins of the Garden of Luxuriance
蒨园遗址

65

Poem-Inscribed Tablet at the Crescent Terrace
The terrace was on a hillock east of the "Vast Vistas of Sea and Mountains." The crescent-shaped white marble balustrades skirted the North Lake and West Lake. It was a place for the Qing emperors to admire the moon, because when the moon was bright at the Mid-Autumn Festival, the scene was like what was described in one of Li Bai's poems. The stone tablet is now in Peking University.

半月台诗碑
半月台在"海岳开襟"东侧土山之上。白玉石为栏，形如半月，襟带北湖和西湖的辽阔水域，中秋月明，大有李白镜湖诗意，是清帝赏月之处。图为乾隆御笔半月台诗碑，今在北京大学内。

Autumn at the Ruins of the Baoxiang Temple
The Baoxiang Temple was a lamaist temple at the North Lake in the Garden of Eternal Spring. It was built on level ground in front of a lake-side hillock. On his return from a tour to the south, Emperor Qianlong had two statues of the Goddess of Mercy made after the Goddess of Mercy in the Faxi Temple in Hangzhou, one enshrined in the Qingliang Buddhist Grotto on the Hill of Jade Spring and the other here.

宝相寺遗址秋色
宝相寺是长春园北湖的喇嘛寺庙，襟山带湖，体势平远。乾隆南巡归来，命仿塑杭州上天竺法喜寺之观音大士像二，一供奉于玉泉山清凉禅窟，一供该寺之中。

Western Buildings

The area of Western Buildings is the most noticeable place at the ruins of Yuanmingyuan. Occupying only seven hectares of land, it is at the northern end of the Garden of Eternal Spring and extended from west to east in 10 groups of structures in the Baroque and Rococo styles of the 18th-century Europe, which included the Building of Exotic Delights, Labyrinth, Bird Cage, Temple of a Another Land, Overseas Hall, House of a Distant Land, Great Fountain, Display Fountain, Parallel Mounds and Parallel View, complete with courtyards and fountains.

西洋楼

西洋楼是圆明园遗址最引人注目的一区,实际面积仅7公顷,地处长春园尽北端,自西向东,包括谐奇趣、黄花阵、养雀笼、方外观、海晏堂、远瀛观、大水法、观水法、浅法山、线法画十组西欧18世纪"巴洛克"、"洛可可"式建筑、庭院和喷泉。

Ruins of the Building of Exotic Delights
This building with fountains was the first one of its kind built in the 16th year of Qianlong (1751) in the style of an Italian villa.

谐奇趣遗址
乾隆十六年（1751）建成的第一座意大利别墅风格的水法殿

A new labyrinth was built in the 1980s on the site of the former Labyrinth.

八十年代于黄花阵遗址上复建的迷宫

Temple of Another Land
Built together with the Overseas Hall in the 24th year of Qianlong (1759), this was once the place where Lady Rong, a favourite Hui concubine of Emperor Qianlong (the legendary Fragrant Lady), performed prayers.

方外观
与海晏堂同建于乾隆二十四年（1759），一度是乾隆回族宠妃"容妃"（传说中的香妃）做礼拜的地方。

This Western-style five-arch bridge in the Temple of Another Land is now in Peking University.
方外观西式五孔桥（现在北京大学内）

Overseas Hall.
海晏堂

73

Water Tower.
蓄水楼

74

◀ Great Fountain.
大水法

Ruins of the House of a
Distant Land.
远瀛观遗址

An ink drawing of the
Great Fountain.
大水法墨线图

Carved stones.

细部雕刻

The stone lions and screen wall at the front gate of Beijing Library came from Yuanmingyuan.

北京图书馆门前的石狮和影壁皆是圆明园旧物

Remains of the foundation of the Pavilion of Floating Cup east of the ruins of the House of a Distant Land.
现存远瀛观遗址东侧的流杯亭基座

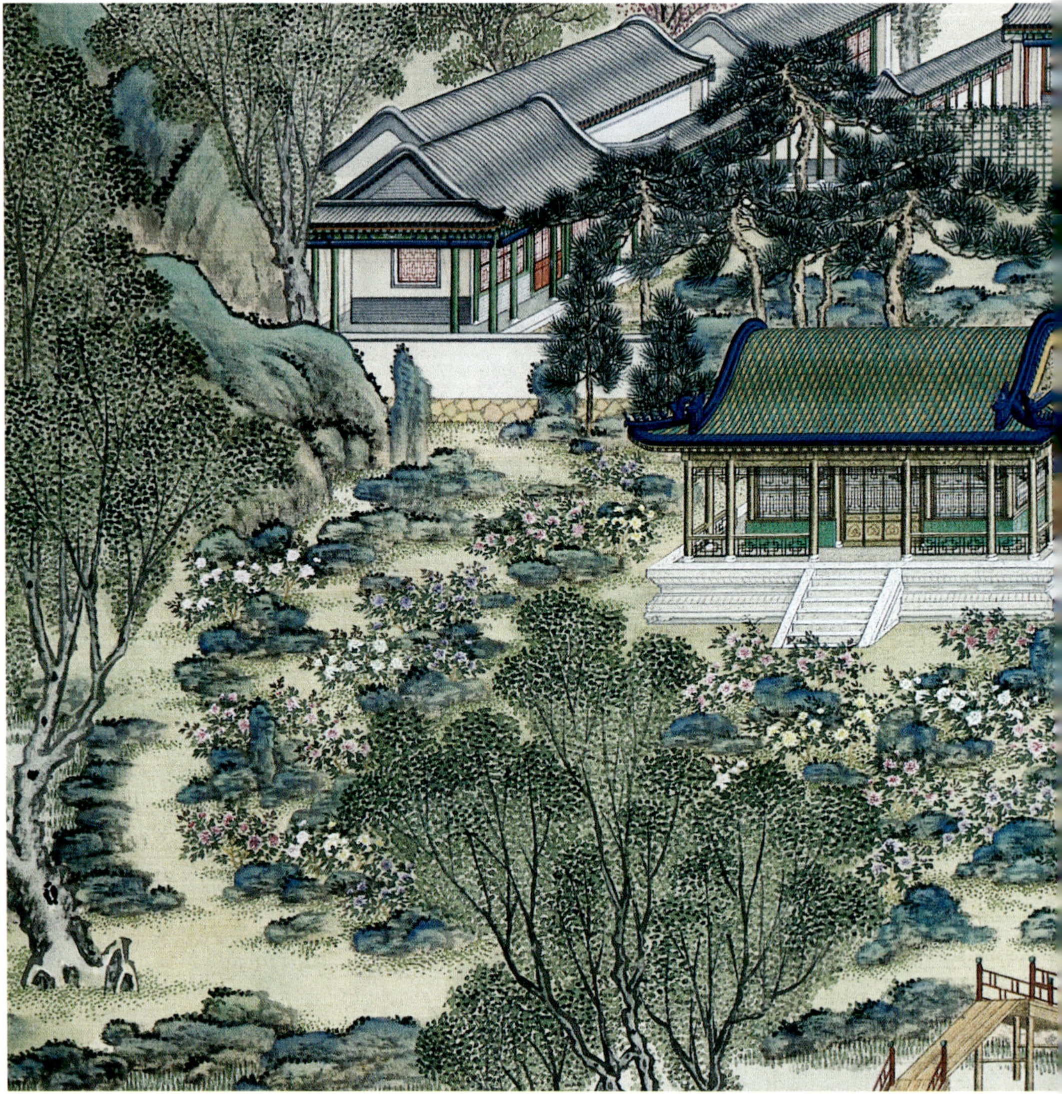

Peony Terrace

This gorgeous structure built of nanmu wood and two-colour glazed roof tiles was already famous at the time of Emperor Kangxi. The hundreds of peonies of many colours planted in front of it were the best of the Three Hills and Five Gardens. In the spring of the 61st year of Kangxi (1722), when Yinzhen (the later Emperor Yongzheng) invited Emperor Kangxi to the garden to look at the peonies, his own 12-year-old son Hongli (the later Emperor Qianlong) also came. It was a gathering of three generations of emperors. When Emperor Qianlong ascended the throne, a memorial hall was built here in honour of his grandfather.

牡丹台

在康熙年间即已著名，殿以香楠为材，覆二色琉璃瓦，焕若金碧。前植牡丹数百本，姚黄魏紫，为三山五园之冠。康熙六十一年（1722）春，当时的皇四子胤禛（后来的雍正）迎奉康熙来园中赏花，年仅12岁的弘历（乾隆）也随侍叩见，祖孙三代天子共聚牡丹台。乾隆即位后，特建纪恩堂以纪念乃祖。

Yongzheng Pursuing Pleasures

This is a set of 14 pictures painted on silk and depicting Yongzheng's life in the garden. The picture reproduced here shows Emperor Yongzheng teasing a small black monkey.

雍正行乐图

绢本设色，绘雍正在园中的生活，共14幅。图中雍正皇帝正在引追一只小黑猴儿。

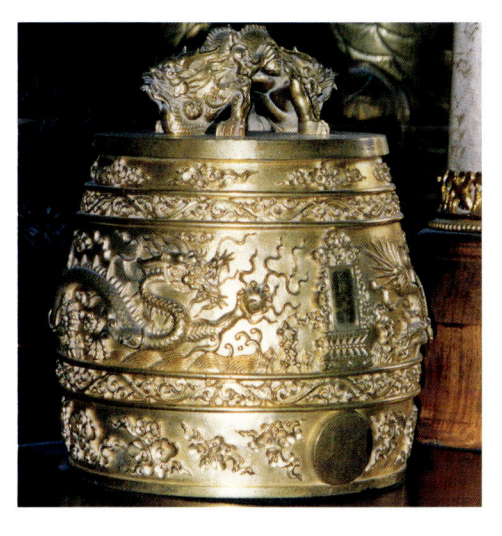

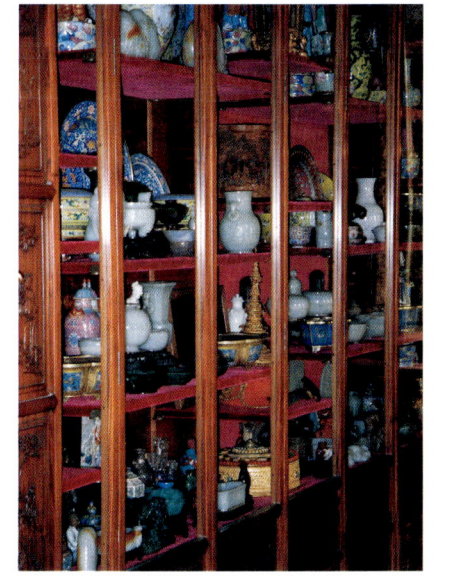

Treasures from Yuanmingyuan in the Fontainebleau Palace of Paris, France.
今藏法国巴黎枫丹白露宫的圆明遗珍

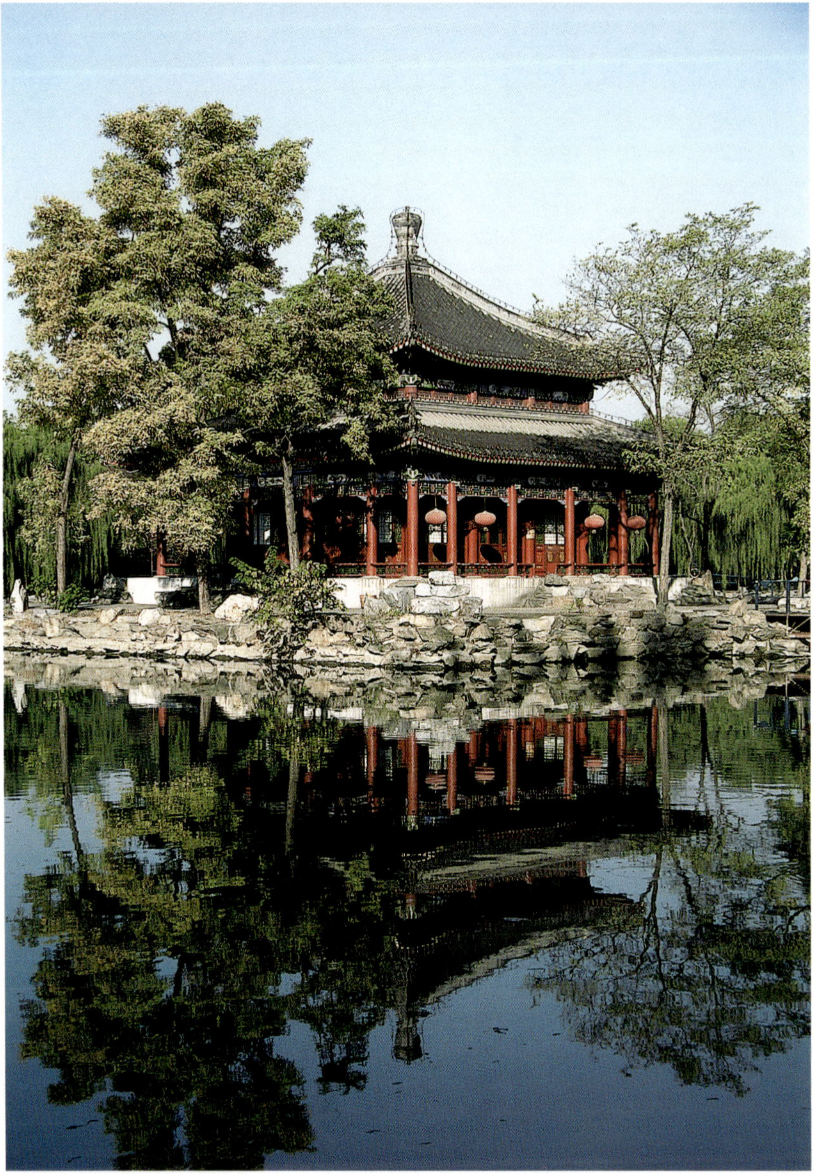

Remains of an arched bridge south of the Green-Mirroring Pavilion in the Garden of Beautiful Spring.
绮春园鉴碧亭南幸存的石拱桥遗址。

◀ The Green-Mirroring Pavilion after restoration.
复修后的鉴碧亭

The newly built Nine-Bend Bridge at the Phoenix and Unicorn Islet in the Garden of Beautiful Spring.

绮春园凤麟洲遗址上新建的九曲桥

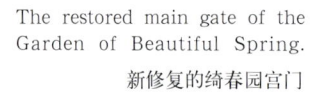

The restored main gate of the Garden of Beautiful Spring.

新修复的绮春园宫门

图书在版编目(CIP)数据

圆明园：英汉对照／朱杰编著. －北京：外文出版社, 2000
ISBN7-119-02627-5

Ⅰ.圆... Ⅱ.朱... Ⅲ.圆明园－画册 Ⅳ.K928.73-64
中国版本图书馆 CIP 数据核字(2000)第 07437 号

Text by: Zhu Jie
Edited by: Lan Peijing
Photos by: Lui Jiwen   Yao Tianxin
　　　　　　　Zhu Jie   Zhou Baoyi
　　　　　　　Luo Guanglin   Chu Zonggang
　　　　　　　Wei Xianwen   Jiang Chao
　　　　　　　Chen Pinshen   Dong Ruichen
　　　　　　　Yuan Yi   Lan Peijing
Translated by: Tang Bowen
Designed by: Yuan Qing

First edition 2000

Yuanmingyuan Garden

ISBN7-119-02627-5

© Foreign Languages Press
Published by Foreign Languages Press
24 Baiwanzhuang Road, Beijing 100037, China
Home Page:http://www.flp.com.cn
E-mail Addresses: info@flp.com.cn
　　　　　　　　　sales@flp.com.cn
Printed in the People's Republic of China

编辑：朱　杰
责任编辑：兰佩瑾
摄影：刘继文　姚天新　朱　杰
　　　邹宝义　罗广林　初宗纲
　　　韦显文　蒋　超　陈平生
　　　董瑞成　袁　一　兰佩瑾
翻译：汤博文
设计：元青

圆 明 园

朱　杰　编

© 外文出版社
外文出版社出版
(中国北京百万庄大街24号)
邮政编码 100037
外文出版社网页：http://www.flp.com.cn
外文出版社电子邮件地址：info@flp.com.cn
　　　　　　　　　　　　sales@flp.com.cn
深圳麟德电脑设计制作有限公司制版
天时印刷（深圳）有限公司印刷
2000年（24开）第一版
2000年第一版第一次印刷
（英汉）
ISBN7-119-02627-5/J.1533（外）
004800（精）